Books of the Bible Puzzlers

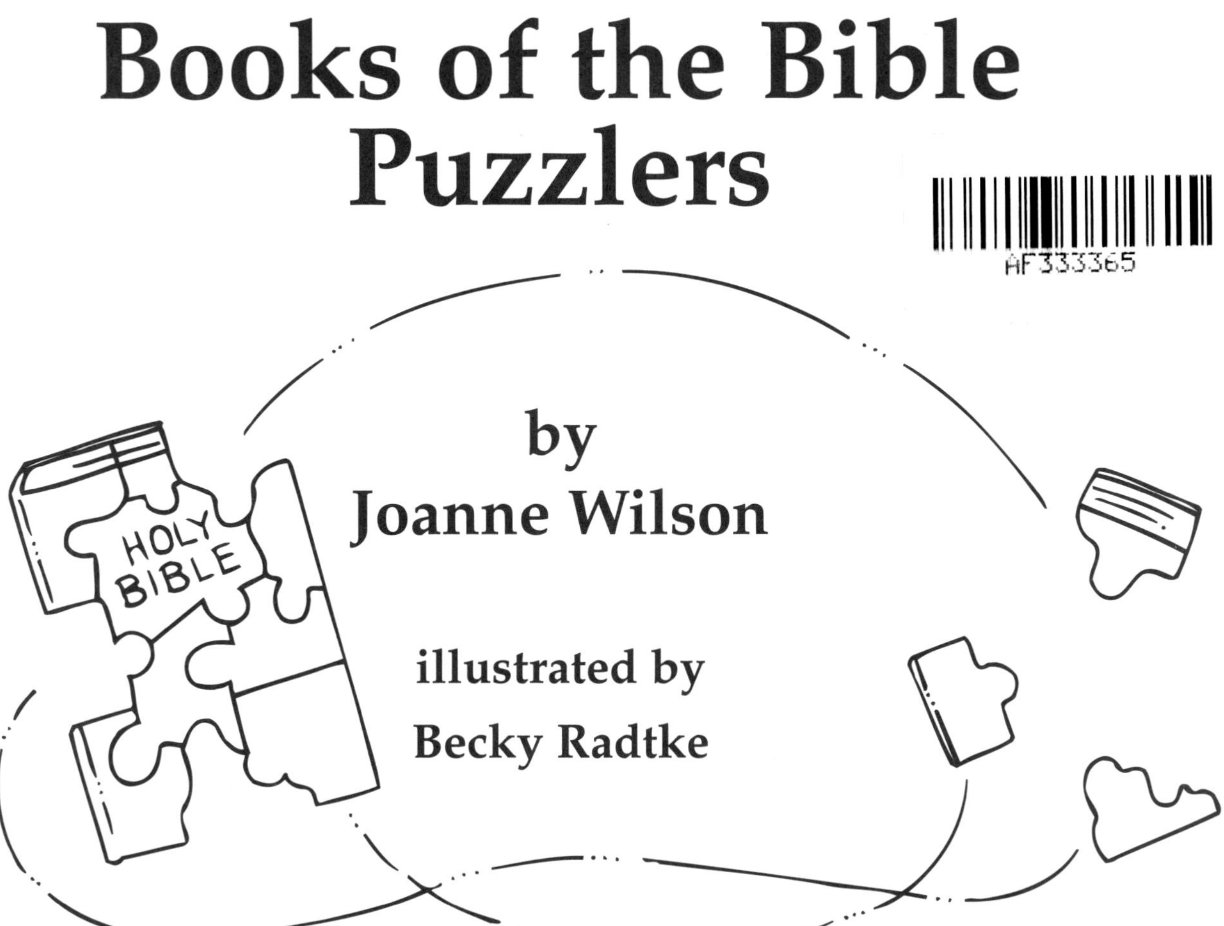

by
Joanne Wilson

illustrated by
Becky Radtke

Cover by Ron Wheeler

Copyright © 1996, Shining Star

ISBN No. 0-382-30701-1

Standardized Subject Code TA ac

Printing No. 98765432

Shining Star
A Division of Frank Schaffer Publications, Inc.
23740 Hawthorne Boulevard
Torrance, CA 90505-5927

Unless otherwise indicated, the New International Version of the Bible was used in preparing the activities in this book.

Table of Contents

Dedication

Dedicated to my husband, a kind and gentle Christian. What a privilege to share my life with him! His support in my writing ministry and his help in proofreading are invaluable.

To Parents and Teachers

Books of the Bible Puzzlers, for grades 4-6, presents the Bible as a library of books. Fun activities teach basic Bible skills of book and reference location through hands-on discovery learning. These experiences provide a foundation for building higher levels of biblical knowledge. Repetition aids in the learning process. The best way to use this book is to begin on page 4 and work through to the end. However, each page stands alone and may be used by itself or as a supplementary activity with your Bible lesson.

Books of the Bible Puzzlers may be used successfully in Sunday school, Bible club, release-time class, family Bible study, or individual learning. Adults as well as children with little knowledge of the Bible will find this book helpful. It is also valuable as a review for dedicated Bible students.

Ten Bible verses are suggested at the end of each page to acquaint the student with sample content from each book of the Bible.

"All Scripture is God-breathed and is useful for teaching, rebuking, correcting and training in righteousness, so that the man of God may be thoroughly equipped for every good work." (2 Timothy 3:16-17)

0-382-30701-1

Bible Library

The Bible is like a library of many books. How many books are there?
Use the table of contents in your Bible to write in the names of the missing books below.

0-382-30701-1

First, Middle, and Last

Follow the arrows. Write the letters you passed at the end of each line.

First Book in the Bible
(Old Testament)

Middle Book in the Bible
(Old Testament)

Last Book in the Bible
(New Testament)

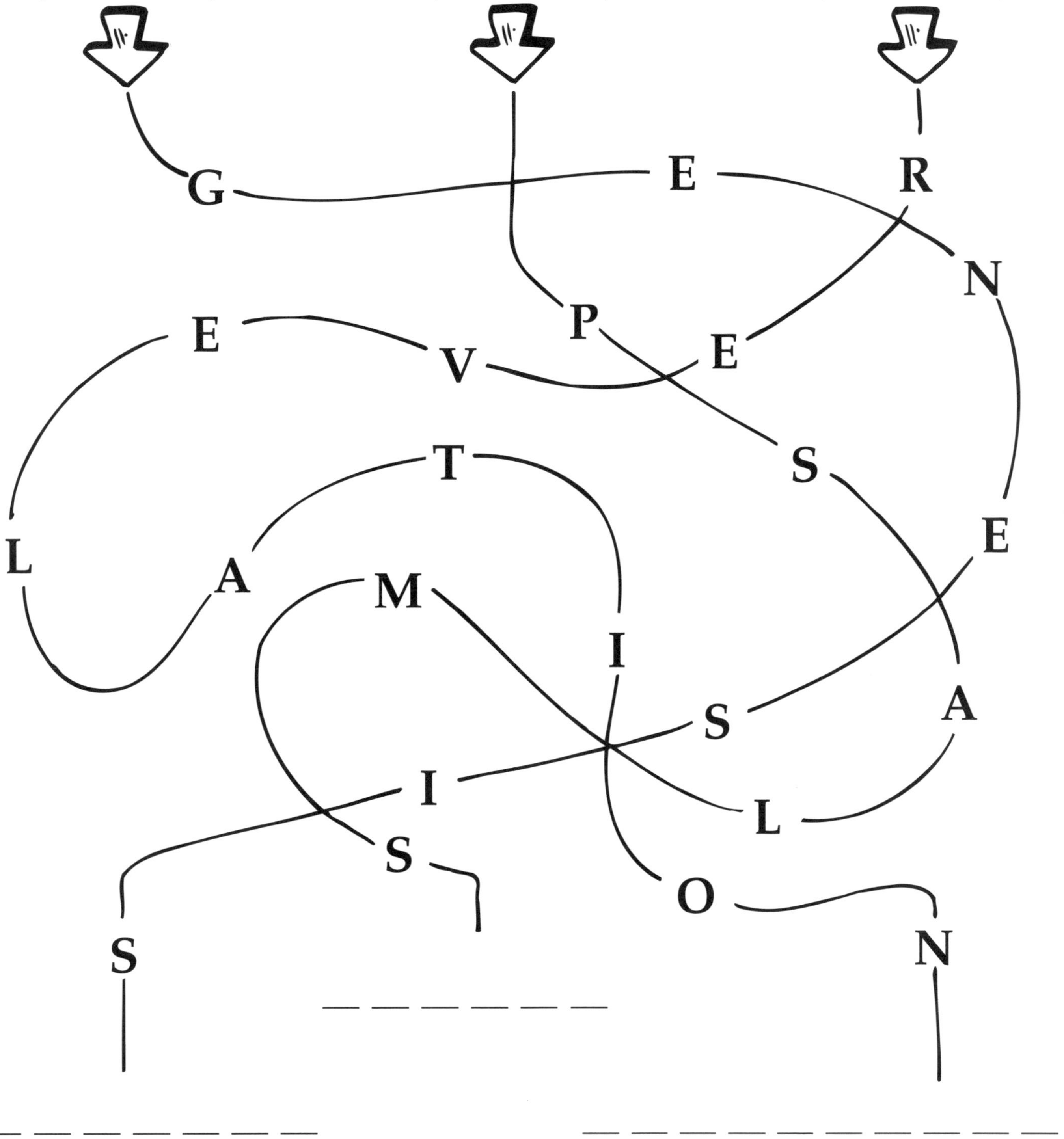

S _ _ _ _ _ _ N

_ _ _ _ _ _ _ _ _ _ _

The Open Bible

0-382-30701-1

What's in Your Bible?

The books of the Bible are printed in the front of most Bibles, in the order in which they are found. (Some Bibles list the books in alphabetical order.) Books can be found easily by looking at this page. The numbers give the location of the first page of each book. Find this list in your Bible.

Below are examples of lists of contents in different Bibles. Circle the one that is the most like the one in your Bible.

Names and Order of Books of the Old and New Testament

	Abbreviation	Page	Chapters
Genesis	Gen.	1	50
Exodus	Ex.	56	40
Leviticus	Lev.	99	27

Contents
Old Testament

Genesis	1
Exodus	49
Leviticus	89
Numbers	121

Contents
Alphabetical List of the Books of the Bible

Acts	925
Amos	747
1 Chronicles	353
2 Chronicles	383
Colossians	1033

Table of Contents
Old Testament

Gen.	1
Ex.	49
Lev.	89
Num.	121

Write the page number on which these books can be found in your Bible from the Table of Contents.

Genesis   page ________

Joshua   page ________

Job   page ________

Isaiah   page ________

Hosea   page ________

Matthew   page ________

Acts   page ________

Romans   page ________

James   page ________

0-382-30701-1

Chapters and Verses

The books in the Bible are divided into chapters. Turn to Genesis. Find chapter 1, chapter 2, and chapter 3. Each chapter is divided into verses by numbers. How many verses are in chapter 1 of Genesis? _______ How many in chapter 2? _______ In 3? _______

Verses in the Bible to be looked up are called Bible references. Below are six Bible references. How are they different? How are they alike?

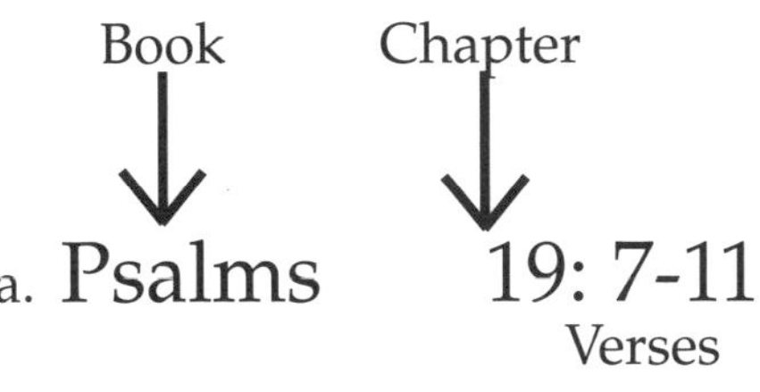

b. Genesis 1:1
c. Revelation 1:3
d. Genesis 1—2
e. Psalms 61:8—62:2
f. Revelation 3:20a

Match a reference above with the words below. Write the letter on the line.

_____ 1. Read the third verse of chapter one.

_____ 2. Read the first part of verse twenty in chapter three.

_____ 3. Read verses seven to eleven of chapter nineteen.

_____ 4. Read the first verse in the first chapter.

_____ 5. Read three verses beginning with verse eight through verse two in the next chapter.

_____ 6. Read chapters one and two.

Write the references on the lines below. The first one is done for you.

7. Verse 89 of chapter 119 of Psalms: _____Psalm 119:89_____

8. Verse 13 of chapter 14 of Revelation: _______________

9. Verses 105 and 130 of chapter 119 of Psalms _______________

READ: Genesis 1:1-2; 2:7-8; Psalm 119:9-12; Revelation 22:18-19.

Divisions of the Old Testament

The Bible has two parts: the Old and the New Testament. *Testament* means: covenant, promise, agreement between God and people.

Write the Bible divisions on the lines.

1. _______________ Genesis, Exodus, Leviticus, Numbers, Deuteronomy: Creation: God's instructions for living together, how to serve and worship God

2. _______________ Joshua, Judges, Ruth, 1 and 2 Samuel, 1 and 2 Kings, 1 and 2 Chronicles, Ezra, Nehemiah, Esther: the story of God's people from their entrance into the promised land to 400 years before Jesus' birth

3. _______________ Job, Psalms, Proverbs, Ecclesiastes, Song of Songs: first written as Hebrew poetry. Psalms was the Hebrew people's hymn book.

4. _______________ _______________ Isaiah, Jeremiah, Lamentations, Ezekiel, Daniel: written by prophets who gave God's messages to His people

5. _______________ _______________ Hosea, Joel, Amos, Obadiah, Jonah, Micah, Nahum, Habakkuk, Zephaniah, Haggai, Zechariah, Malachi: written by prophets who gave God's message to His people.

The books in this chart are out of order. Place them in the correct division with a check mark. The first one is done for you.

	Law	History	Poetry	Major Prophets	Minor Prophets
1. Amos					✔
2. Genesis					
3. Malachi					
4. Joshua					
5. Job					
6. Daniel					
7. Exodus					
8. Haggai					
9. Isaiah					
10. Numbers					
11. Ezra					
12. Psalms					

Genesis

Key verse: Genesis. 1:1   Genesis means ___ ___ ___ ___ ___ ___ ___ ___ ___ .

Label the sections of the time line, using words from the word box.

___ ___ ___ ___ ___ ___ ___ ___   ___ ___ ___   ___ ___ ___ ___
Adam and Eve   Adam and Eve   Noah

___ ___ ___ ___ ___   ___ ___ ___ ___ ___ ___ ___ ___ ___
Different languages   Beginning of the Hebrew Nation

READ: Genesis 37:23, 28; 50:15, 17, 19-21, 24-26.

	Genesis
L	Exodus
A	Leviticus
W	Numbers
	Deuteronomy

Exodus

Key verse: Exodus 13:14   Exodus means ___ ___ ___ ___ ___   ___ ___ ___

Label the sections of the time line, using words from the word box.

Exodus 1-2	**2-4**	**7-12**	**12-13**

_ _ _ _ _ _ _ _ _ _ _ _

in Egypt

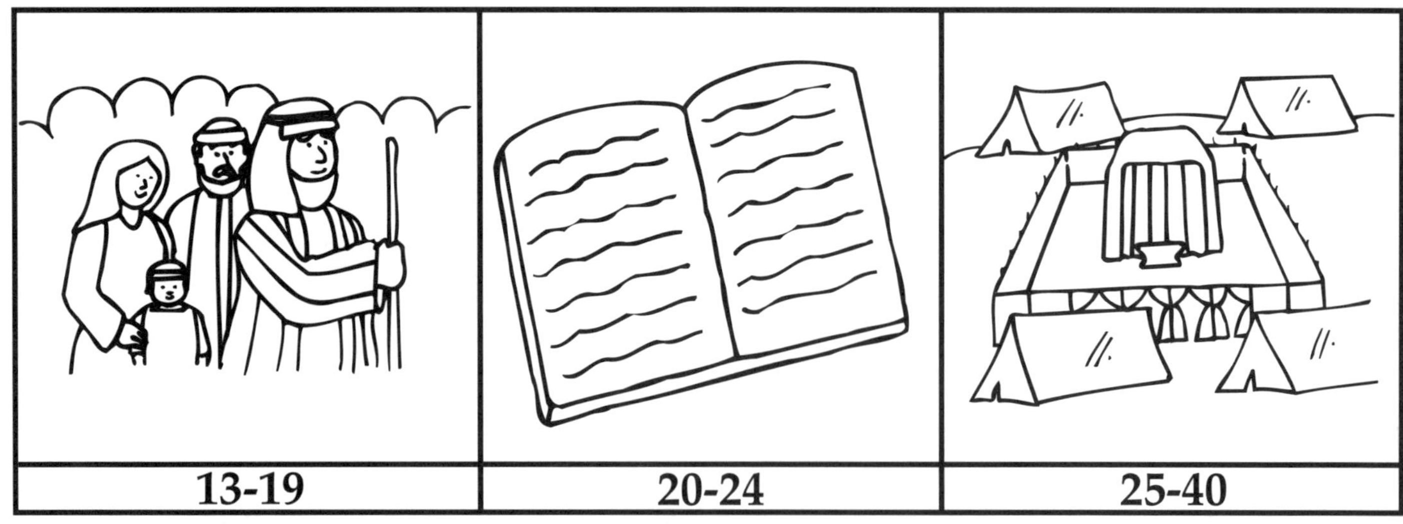

13-19	**20-24**	**25-40**

_ _ _ _ _ _   _ _ _   _ _ _ _ _ _ _ _ _ _ _

                                                    and sacrifice

of Egypt   and other laws

READ: Genesis 12:1-3; 15:12-14; 22:17-18; Exodus 13:17-18.

Leviticus; Numbers

	Genesis
L	Exodus
A	Leviticus
W	Numbers
	Deuteronomy

Leviticus

Key verse: Leviticus 19:2.   Key Word: ___ ___ ___ ___

God appointed the Levities to be religious leaders. God's instructions for worship included

___ ___ ___ ___ ___ ___ ___ ___ ___ and ___ ___ ___ ___ ___ ___ ___ ___ ___ ___. God gave

His people instructions for how to live.

Numbers

Key Verse: Numbers 1:1   Key word: ___ ___ ___ ___ ___ ___

Moses numbered (counted) the Israelites in chapters 1 and 26.

Moses sent one man from each of the twelve tribes to search Canaan. They brought back grapes, pomegranates, and figs. Ten men gave a bad report. Two explorers believed God would help them enter Canaan.

Find on this bunch of grapes the hidden names of the two brave men.
Write the letters from grapes 1, 3, 5, 7, and 9 on line A.
Write the letters from grapes 2, 4, 6, 8, 10, and 11 on line B.

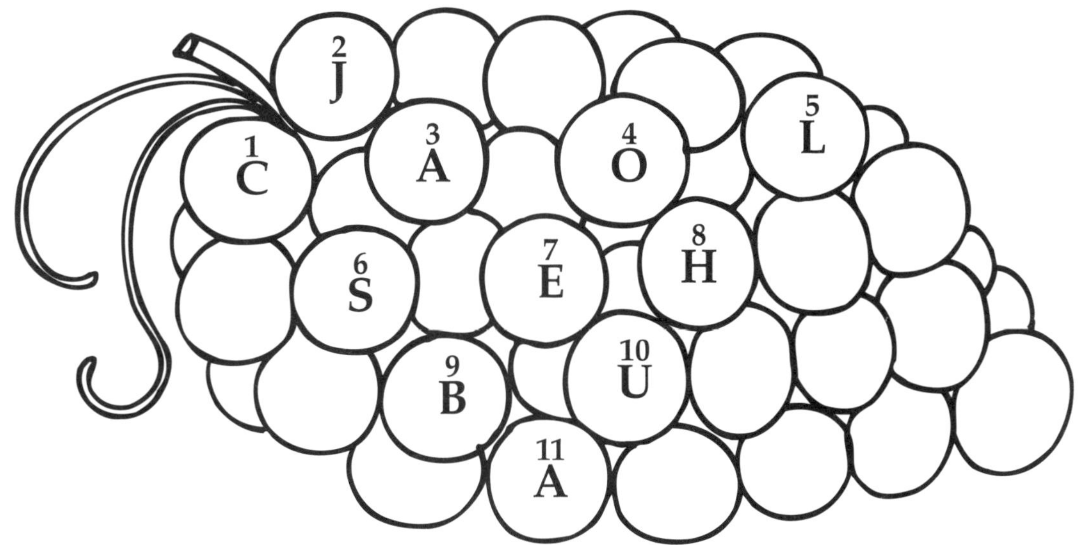

A. ___ ___ ___ ___ ___   B. ___ ___ ___ ___ ___ ___

The people did not ___ ___ ___ ___ God. They would not go into ___ ___ ___ ___ ___ ___. They

wandered in the wilderness ___ ___ ___ ___ ___ years.

READ: Numbers 13:1,17-20,33; 14:36-38; 36:13.

Numbers

The Israelites wandered in the wilderness for forty years. Begin at Kadesh and find the way through the maze to Mount Nebo. Read the verses as you pass them.

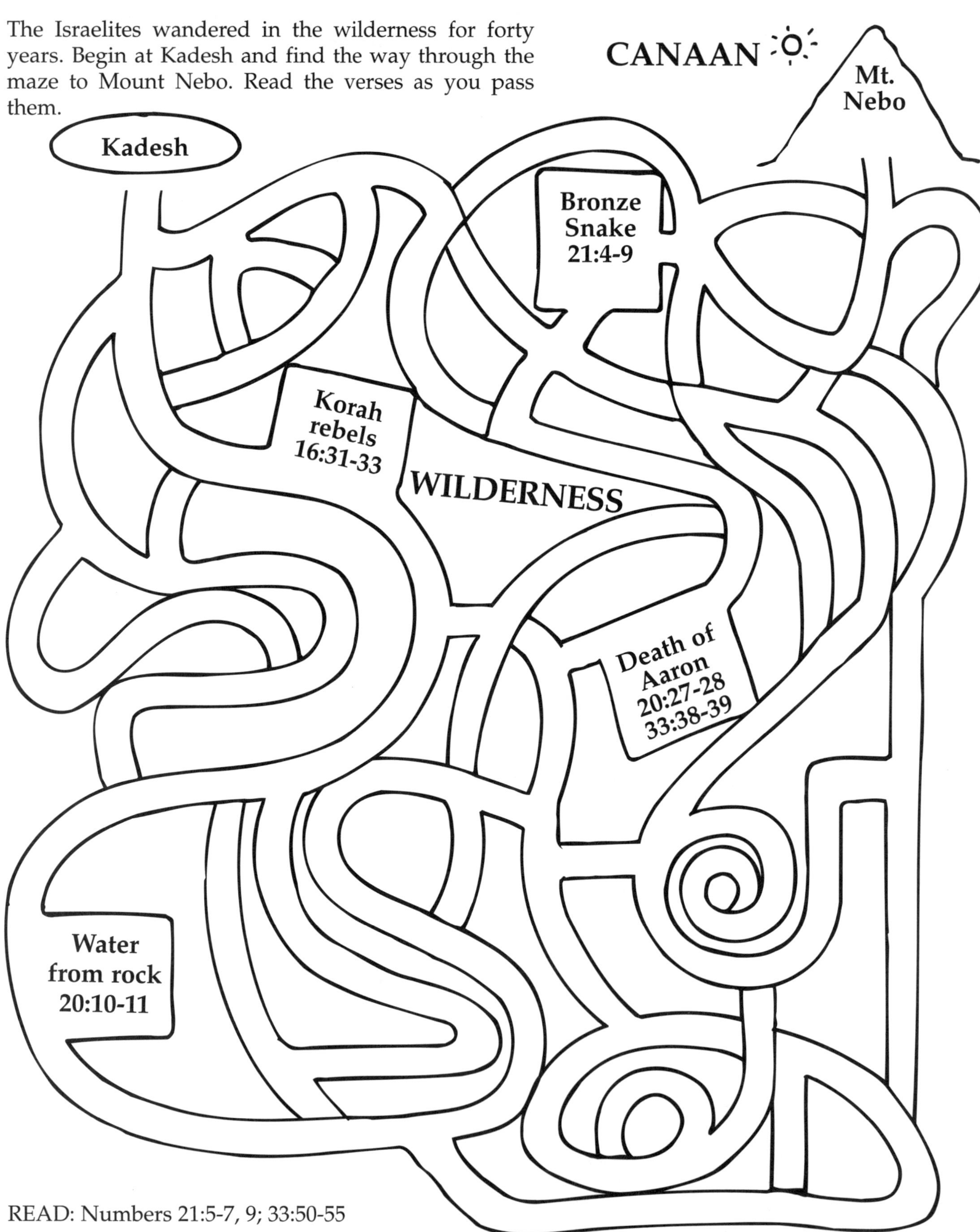

READ: Numbers 21:5-7, 9; 33:50-55

Deuteronomy

	A	B
1	slaves	God
2	Pharaoh	wilderness
3	Egypt	sinned
4	Covenant	days
5	Remember	Abraham

L	Genesis
A	Exodus
W	Leviticus
	Numbers
	Deuteronomy

Deuteronomy: The law was repeated before God's people entered the Promised Land. Use the code to complete this page.

KEY WORD: <u>Remember</u>
      A5

Chapters 1–4: _______________ the Hebrew history.
           A5
Chapters 5–26: _______________ the Hebrew law.
           A5
Chapters 23–30: _______________ the covenant.
           A5
Chapters 31–34: _______________ God's faithfulness on the journey from Egypt to Canaan.
           A5

____
    A5
you were _______________ in _______________ and _______________ brought you out.
        A1   A3   B1
what _______________ did to _______________ in _______________.
     B1   A2   A3
_______________ led you through the _______________ (8:2).
   B1   B2
the _______________ _______________ made with you (8:18).
    A4   B1
how you _______________ in the desert.
       B3
_______________, Isaac, and Jacob.
  B5
the time you left _______________.
       A3

READ: Deuteronomy 1:21-26; 5:15; 34:9-11.

Joshua; Judges; Ruth

<table>
<tr><td rowspan="11">H
I
S
T
O
R
Y</td><td>Joshua</td></tr>
<tr><td>Judges</td></tr>
<tr><td>Ruth</td></tr>
<tr><td>1 Samuel</td></tr>
<tr><td>2 Samuel</td></tr>
<tr><td>1 Kings</td></tr>
<tr><td>2 Kings</td></tr>
<tr><td>1 Chronicles</td></tr>
<tr><td>2 Chronicles</td></tr>
<tr><td>Ezra</td></tr>
<tr><td>Nehemiah</td></tr>
</table>

Esther

Joshua

Number the sentences according to the length of the line under the first word. You'll discover what the Book of Joshua is about.

____ Crossing Jordan River   ____ Enemies destroyed

____ Joshua becomes leader   ____ Land given to families

____ Moses dies   ____ Cities of refuge

____ Joshua dies   ____ Walls of Jericho fall

Use words from the word box to complete information about Joshua and Judges.

Joshua knew that true success depends on __ __ __ __ __ __ __ the __ __ __ __ of God.

In the days of Judges, the people went in circles.

They __ __ __ __ __ __ __ __ __ God.

They were

__ __ __ __ __ __ __ __ __ by enemies.

Word Box

God	obeying
defeated	disobeyed
prayed	Word

__ __ __ sent them a judge.

They

__ __ __ __ __ __ to God for help.

Judges

Unscramble three of the best known judges.

R B D H A O E 4:4 ___________________

D O E N G I 6:11 ___________________

M S A O N S 13:24 ___________________

Ruth

Number these events in order according to the length of the line under the first word. You'll discover what the Book of Ruth is about.

____ Jesus will become a distant relative of Ruth.

____ Ruth goes to Canaan with her mother-in-law, Naomi.

____ Ruth marries Boaz.

____ Ruth gathers grain in the field of Boaz.

____ Ruth lives in Moab.

READ: Joshua 1:1-2, 6-8; Judges 2:16-19; Ruth 1:16.

1 and 2 Samuel

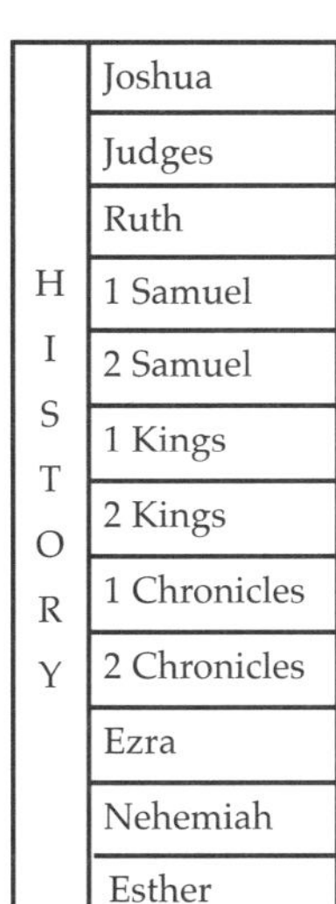

1 Samuel: End of Judges' rule. Forming of the Kingdom of Israel.

2 Samuel: Kingship of David.

To find the main characters in these two books, place your pencil on the letter square with the same number as the activity. Draw a line, going from one letter to another, until you spell out the names.

1. ____Samuel____ was the last judge. He said, "To _____________ is better than _____________." (Read 1 Samuel 15:22 to find the answer.)

2. _____________ was the first king of Israel. (1 Samuel 9-10)

3. _____________ killed Goliath, the giant (1 Samuel 17) and became Israel's second king.

4. _____________, the prophet, reminded the second king of his sin. (2 Samuel 12:1-14)

5. _____________ was the son of the first king and the best friend of the second king of Israel. (1 Samuel 19:1)

6. _____________ was the son of the second king. (2 Samuel 15-18)

READ: 1 Samuel 3:8-10; 12:14,15; 16:7; 2 Samuel 23:2-5.

1 and 2 Kings; 1 and 2 Chronicles

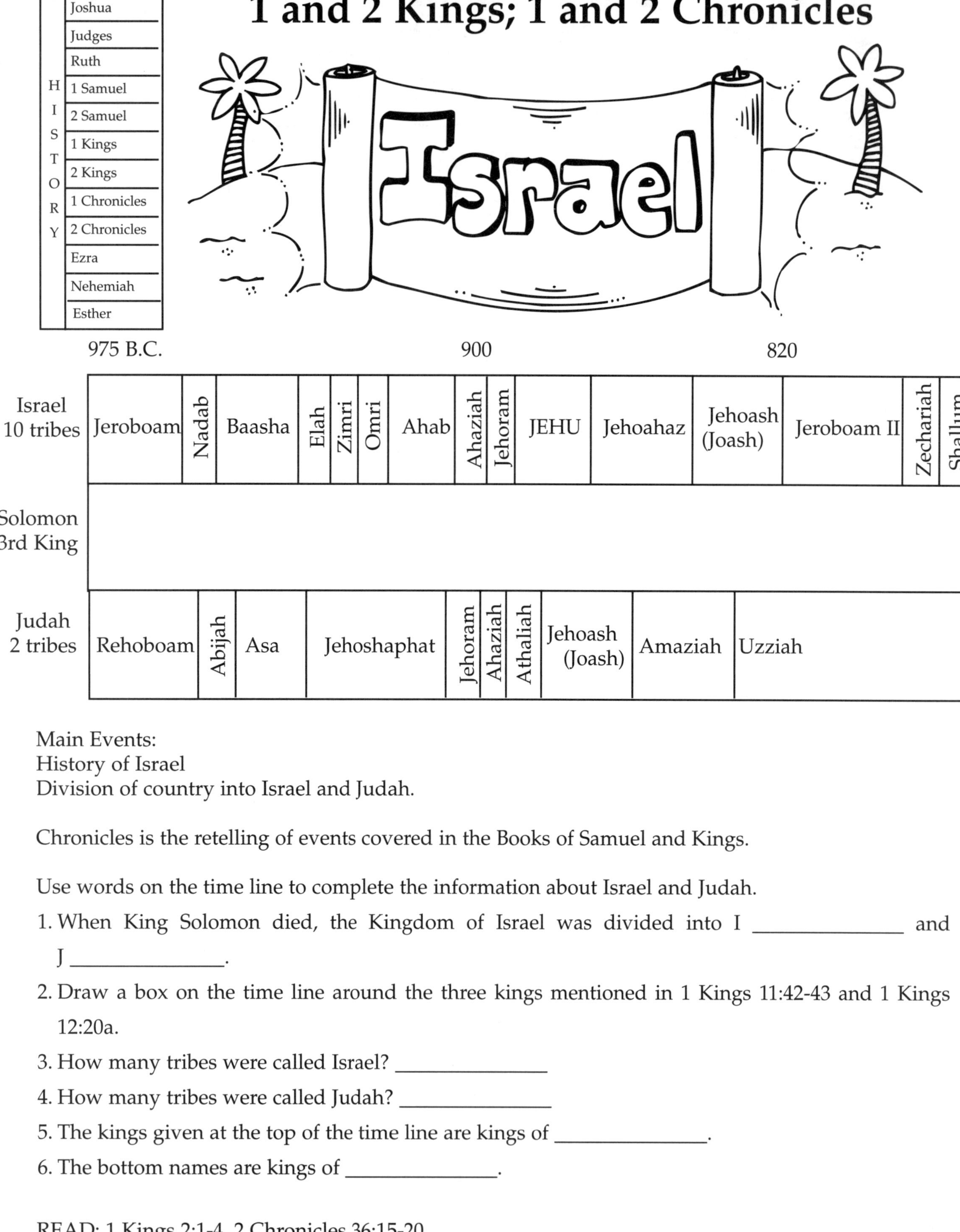

Timeline

	975 B.C.							900					820	
Israel 10 tribes	Jeroboam	Nadab	Baasha	Elah	Zimri	Omri	Ahab	Ahaziah / Jehoram	JEHU	Jehoahaz	Jehoash (Joash)	Jeroboam II	Zechariah	Shallum
Solomon 3rd King														
Judah 2 tribes	Rehoboam	Abijah	Asa	Jehoshaphat	Jehoram / Ahaziah / Athaliah		Jehoash (Joash)	Amaziah	Uzziah					

Main Events:
History of Israel
Division of country into Israel and Judah.

Chronicles is the retelling of events covered in the Books of Samuel and Kings.

Use words on the time line to complete the information about Israel and Judah.

1. When King Solomon died, the Kingdom of Israel was divided into I ______________ and J ______________.

2. Draw a box on the time line around the three kings mentioned in 1 Kings 11:42-43 and 1 Kings 12:20a.

3. How many tribes were called Israel? ______________

4. How many tribes were called Judah? ______________

5. The kings given at the top of the time line are kings of ______________.

6. The bottom names are kings of ______________.

READ: 1 Kings 2:1-4, 2 Chronicles 36:15-20.

Kings of Israel   722 BC

Menahem	Pekahiah	Pekah	anarchy	Hoshea

Israel taken captive by Assyria

Fall of Jerusalem

Kings of Judah   586 B.C.

Uzziah	Jotham	Ahaz	Hezekiah	Manasseh	Amon	Jehoahaz	Jehoiakim	Jehoiachin	Zedekiah

EXILE for 70 years

Judah taken captive by Babylon

7. The Northern Kingdom of Israel was taken captive by A________________.

8. Who was king in Judah when Israel fell? H________________

9. What king followed Hezekiah? M________________

10. Who was king longer, Hezekiah or Ahaz? ________________

11. What year was Jerusalem destroyed? ________________

12. How long were the Jewish people in exile in Babylon? ________________

13. How many years were between the overthrow of Israel and that of Judah? ________________

READ: 2 Kings 24:18-25:7.

Ezra; Nehemiah; Esther

Ezra

Look up the Bible verses to complete the information about Ezra, Nehemiah ,and Esther.

1. Ezra was a t________________ from Babylon. (Ezra 7:6)

2. Ezra knew the L______________ of ______________. (Ezra 7:6, 10)

3. ______________ was with Ezra. (Ezra 7:6, 9)

4. Ezra returned to Jerusalem in the seventh year of King ______________. (Ezra 7:7)

5. Ezra's journey took ______________ months. (Ezra 7:9)

Nehemiah

Thirteen years after Ezra returned to Jerusalem, Nehemiah returned also.

6. The ______________ of Jerusalem were broken down. (Nehemiah 1:3)

7. The ______________ had been burned. (Nehemiah 1:3)

8. It took ______________ days to rebuild the wall. (Nehemiah 6:15)

9. ______________ read the Law to the people. (Nehemiah 8:5)

Esther

The book of Esther records the deliverance of the Jews by the courage of Queen Esther, a Jewish girl.

10. God used Esther to save the Jewish people from destruction. Her cousin, ______________, told her, "And who knows but that you have come to royal position for such a time as this?" (Esther 4:12-14)
Through Esther's courage, God protected the family line of the promised Savior, ______________ ______________.

READ: Nehemiah 8:1-10.

Job

Code		
	A	**B**
1	God	Satan
2	person	trouble
3	power	suffering
4	devil	better
5	send	uses

<table>
<tr><td>P</td><td>Job</td></tr>
<tr><td>O</td><td>Psalms</td></tr>
<tr><td>E</td><td>Proverbs</td></tr>
<tr><td>T</td><td>Ecclesiastes</td></tr>
<tr><td>R</td><td></td></tr>
<tr><td>Y</td><td>Song of Songs</td></tr>
</table>

Use the code to complete the lessons we can learn from the Book of Job.

1. ________________, the ________________, has great ________________.
    1B   4A   3A

2. ________________ has greater ________________ than ________________.
    1A   3A   1B

3. ________________ does not ________________ ________________; ________________ does.
    1A   5A   2B   1B

4. ________________ ________________ ________________ and ________________ to make me a
    1A   5B   2B   3B

________________ ________________.
    4B   2A

READ: Job 1:8-12; 2:4-6; 13:15a; 42:12.

Psalms

Use the words next to the musical notes to complete the puzzle.

Across

1. Psalms is a book of P______________.
5. Psalms is the middle book of the B______________.
7. Psalms 113-118 were sung during the P______________.
10. A word that appears many times in the Psalms is r______________.
11. Hebrews used Psalms as a book of w______________.
13. Many Psalms are about J______________.
14. He wrote some of the Psalms. A______________
15. The r______________ of many psalms was lost when they were translated into other languages.
16. Psalms 135-139 are psalms of t______________.

Down

2. Hallelujah means "Praise the L______________."
3. Psalms 2; 45; 72; 110; and 132:11 foretell Jesus as a K______________.
4. Psalms was first written in the language of the______________.
6. He wrote most of the Psalms. D______________.
8. Psalm 16 foretells the r______________ of Jesus.
9. Psalms 22; 41; 55:12-14; and 69:20-21 foretell the s______________ of Jesus.
12. The Psalms were first written as p______________.

READ: Psalms 8:1, 3-4; 23:1-6; 48:14.

Proverbs; Ecclesiastes; Song of Songs

<table>
<tr><td>P</td><td>Job</td></tr>
<tr><td>O</td><td>Psalms</td></tr>
<tr><td>E</td><td>Proverbs</td></tr>
<tr><td>T</td><td>Ecclesiastes</td></tr>
<tr><td>R</td><td>Song of Songs</td></tr>
<tr><td>Y</td><td></td></tr>
</table>

These three books were written by King Solomon. Write all the letters under
1 for Proverbs; 2 for Ecclesiastes; and 3 for Song of Songs. You'll find out what
each book is about.

```
1 2 2 3 2 1 3 2 2 1 3 3 2 1 2 1 2 3 1 3 2 2
A A l A e c l s s o o v o l n l f e e s r o

3 2 1 3 3 1 3 2 1 2 3 2 1 2 1 2 3 1 2 3 2 2
o m c n g t w l i i r f o e n O i o b t e y

1 2 3 1 2 2 3 1 2 3 2 3 1 2 3 2 1 2 3 1 2 2
f i t w n g e i G n o f s d o i e s r s w h

3 1 2 3 2 1 2 1 3 2 1 2 3 1 2 2 1 2 2 3 2 2
h a a i t y r i s e n a w g l l s y c i o u

3 2 3 2 2
f n e t s
```

1. Proverbs: ____

____.

2. Eccelsiastes: _____________________________________:

____

____.

3. Song of Solomon: _________________________________

____

READ: Proverbs 1:7-8; 2:1-5; Eccelsiastes 12:13-14. Song of Songs 1:1.

<table>
<tr><td>

M
A
J
O
R

P
R
O
P
H
E
T
S

</td><td>

Isaiah
Jeremiah
Lamentations
Ezekiel
Daniel

</td></tr>
</table>

Isaiah; Jeremiah; Lamentations

The first five books of prophecy are called Major Prophets. The first one was written by Isaiah. The second and third were written by Jeremiah. All three are about the fall of the Hebrew nation.

Look up the Bible verses. Draw a line from each event on the left to the verse that refers to it.

ISAIAH told about the coming of the Messiah (Savior).

1. His birth   Isaiah 11:1

2. His family   Isaiah 7:14; 9:6

3. Holy Spirit in Him   Isaiah 25:8

4. What He would be like Isaiah 32:1

5. His suffering and death Isaiah 11:2

6. His resurrection   Isaiah 11:5

7. His reign as King   Isaiah 53:5

JEREMIAH told about the coming of the Babylonian army.

8. People taken to their enemies' land for 70 years Jeremiah 32:37-38

9. Promise of returning to Judah Jeremiah 29:10

10. Reason for the Jews' trouble Jeremiah 31:31

11. Promise of a new covenant Jeremiah 25:8-9

For forty years Jeremiah warned the people to turn from their evil ways. They would not listen. He wrote LAMENTATIONS because he knew Jerusalem would be destroyed and the Temple burned. The word *Lamentations* means "to cry out loud."

READ: Isaiah 1:16-20; Jeremiah 11:6-8; Lamentations 3:22-23.

Ezekiel; Daniel

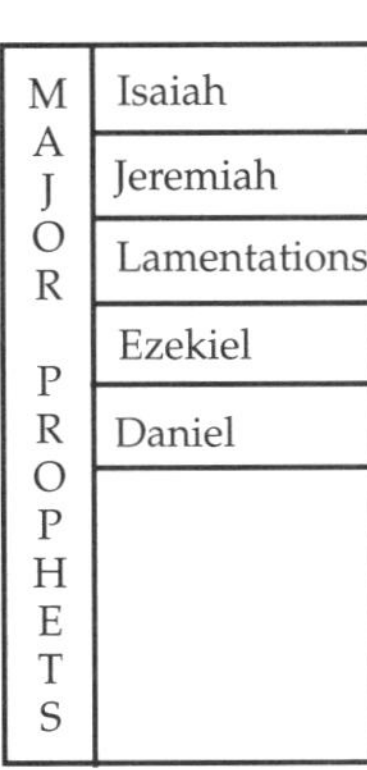

The books of Ezekiel and Daniel were written by men of those names. Both prophets were taken to Babylon as captives. Who was king of Judah when the kingdom of Israel was taken captive by Assyria.? Unscramble his name. Z H H A E I E K

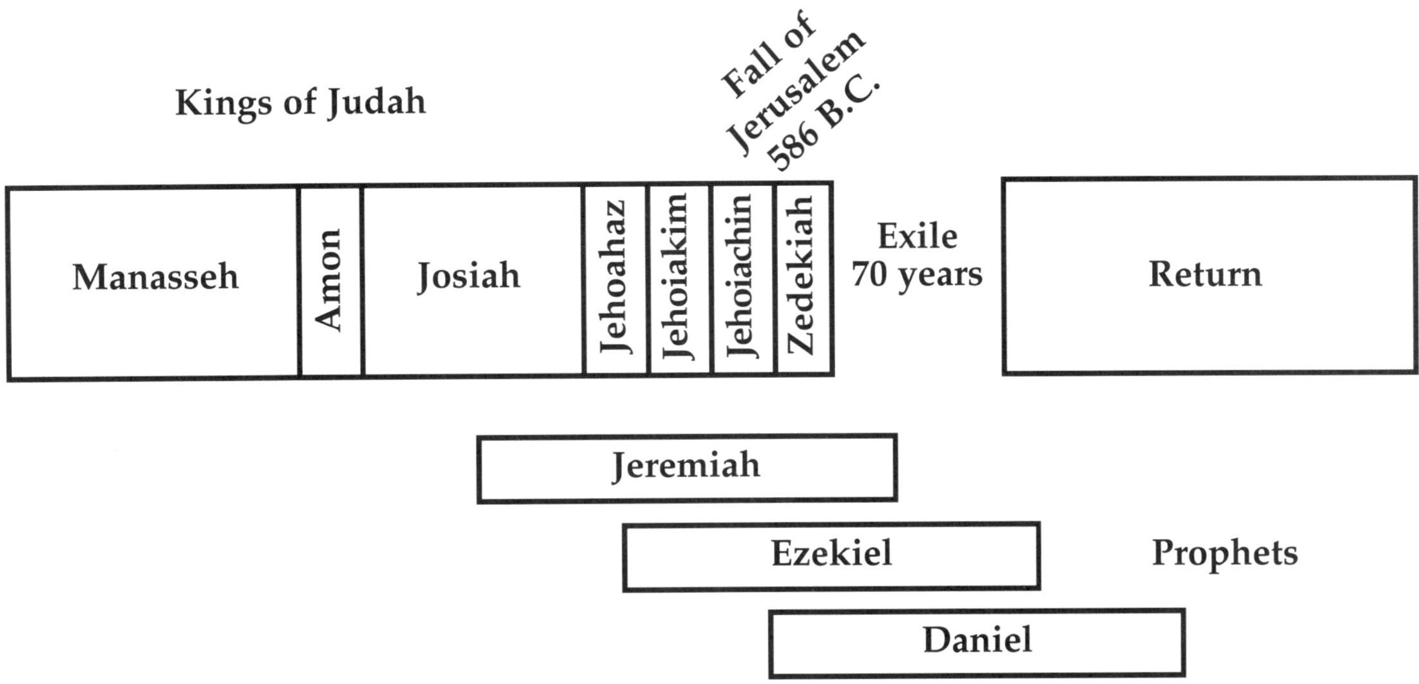

Answer these questions with words from the time line.

1. What prophets were preaching when Jerusalem was destroyed? Three are given. Other prophets also preached at this time. ______________ ______________ ______________

2. How many years were the Jews in exile? Exile means taken from home, forced to stay in another place or country. ______________

3. Who was king when Jeremiah began his ministry? ______________

4. Who was king when Daniel was taken to Babylon? (Daniel 1:2) ______________

READ: Ezekiel 1:2; 2:1-5; Daniel 1:1,3-5.

Hosea; Joel; Amos; Obadiah

M	Hosea
I	Joel
N	Amos
O	Obadiah
R	Jonah
P	Micah
R	Nahum
O	Habakkuk
P	Zephaniah
H	Haggai
E	Zechariah
T	
S	Malachi

Each Minor Prophet book is named after the man who wrote it. The first seven prophets lived many years before Jeremiah, Ezekiel, and Daniel.

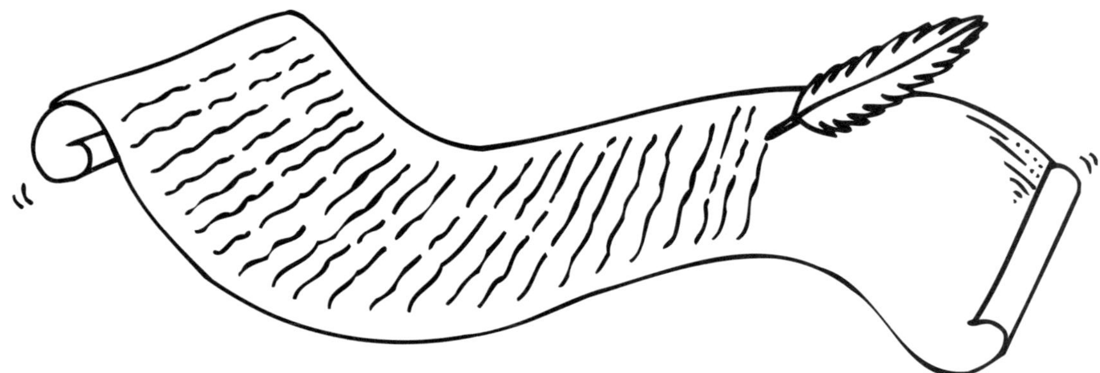

Find the books in which the following words are found. (Hint: Use only the first four Minor Prophets.) The chapter and verse numbers are provided.

Word Hunt

1. Earthquake __ __ __ __ (1:1)

2. Locusts __ __ __ __ (7:1)

3. Vine __ __ __ __ __ (10:1)

4. Edom __ __ __ __ __ __ __ (1:1a)

5. Call __ __ __ __ (2:32a)

6. Basket of fruit __ __ __ __ (8:2)

7. Married Gomer __ __ __ __ __ (1:3)

8. Plumb line __ __ __ __ (7:8)

9. Said, "And everyone who calls on the name of the Lord

   will be saved." __ __ __ __ (2:32a)

READ: Hosea 14:1-2, 9c; Joel 1:1; Amos 1:1a; 7:14-15; Obadiah 1:1-4.

0-382-30701-1

Jonah; Micah; Nahum; Habakkuk

M	Hosea
I	Joel
N	Amos
O	Obadiah
R	Jonah
P	Micah
R	Nahum
O	Habakkuk
P	Zephaniah
H	Haggai
E	Zechariah
T	Zephaniah
S	Malachi

Learn about these four Minor Prophets by adding or subtracting letters from the alphabet as directed. Write the correct letters on the lines.

A B C D E F G H I J K L M N O P Q R S T U V W X Y Z

1. ___ ___ ___ ___ ___   He told where Jesus would be born. (5:2)
   N-1 H+1 A+2 D-3 F+2

2. ___ ___ ___ ___ ___   Jesus talked about him in Matthew 12:40.
   L-2 P-1 Q-3 D-3 K-3

3. ___ ___ ___ ___ ___   He foretold the destruction of Ninevah. (1:1)
   Q-3 E-4 I-1 V-1 J+3

4. ___ ___ ___ ___ ___ ___ ___ ___   He said, ". . . the righteous will live
   J-2 C-2 D-2 B-1 J+1 L-1 V-1 H+3   by his faith." (2:4b)

5. ___ ___ ___ ___ ___   God told him to go to Ninevah, but he went another way. (1:3a)
   K-1 M+2 0-1 C-2 F+2

6. ___ ___ ___ ___ ___   He said, "The Lord is good, a refuge in times of trouble." (1:7a)
   Q-3 E-4 I-1 X-3 J+3

7. ___ ___ ___ ___ ___ ___ ___ ___   He complained to God about
   G+1 B-1 C-1 D-3 I+2 M-2 T+1 H+3   unbelievers. (1:2-4)

8. ___ ___ ___ ___ ___   He said God would forgive sin. (7:18-19)
   0-2 G+2 F-3 C-2 K-3

9. ___ ___ ___ ___ ___   He said, "He (God) cares for those who trust in him." (1:7b)
   R-4 C-2 E+3 T+1 L+1

10. ___ ___ ___ ___ ___ ___ ___ ___   He said, "I will be joyful in God
    G+1 D-3 F-4 B-1 L-1 J+1 W-2 N-3   my Savior." (3:18)

READ: Jonah 1:1-3; 2:1,10; Micah 6:8; 7:18-19; Nahum 1:7; Habakkuk 3:18.

    0-382-30701-1

Zephaniah; Haggai; Zechariah; Malachi

M	Hosea
I	Joel
N	Amos
O	Obadiah
R	Jonah
P	Micah
R	Nahum
O	Habakkuk
P	Zephaniah
H	Haggai
E	Zechariah
T	
S	Malachi

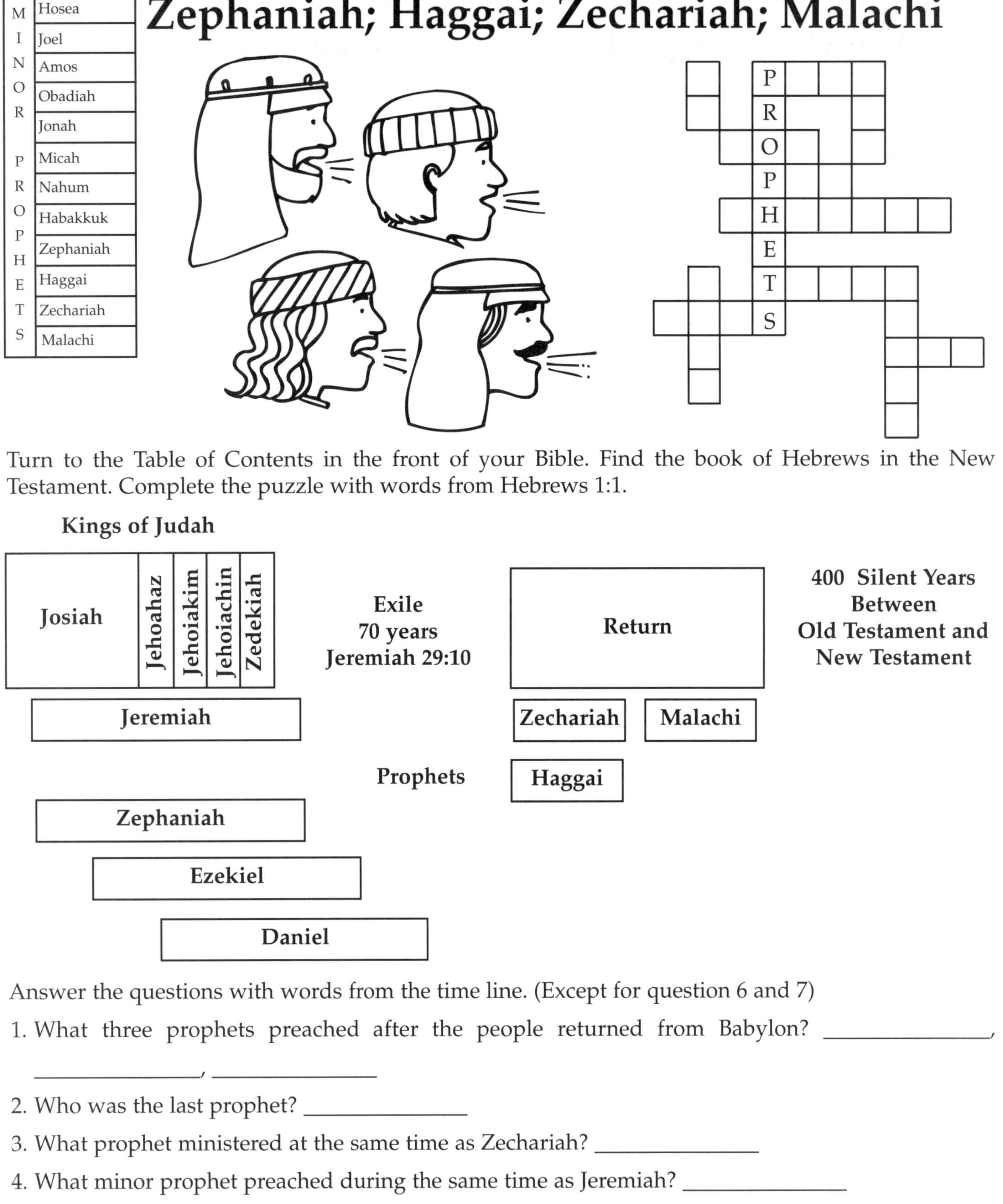

Turn to the Table of Contents in the front of your Bible. Find the book of Hebrews in the New Testament. Complete the puzzle with words from Hebrews 1:1.

Kings of Judah

| Josiah | Jehoahaz | Jehoiakim | Jehoiachin | Zedekiah |

Jeremiah

**Exile
70 years
Jeremiah 29:10**

Return

Zechariah   **Malachi**

**400 Silent Years
Between
Old Testament and
New Testament**

Prophets   **Haggai**

Zephaniah

Ezekiel

Daniel

Answer the questions with words from the time line. (Except for question 6 and 7)

1. What three prophets preached after the people returned from Babylon? _______________, _______________, _______________

2. Who was the last prophet? _______________

3. What prophet ministered at the same time as Zechariah? _______________

4. What minor prophet preached during the same time as Jeremiah? _______________

5. How many years were the people in Babylon? _______________

6. How many Minor Prophet books are in the Bible? _______________

7. How many Major Prophet books are in the Bible? _______________

READ: Zephaniah 3:17; Haggai 2:4-5; Zechariah 1:1-4; Malachi 3:10, 12; 4:4.

Divisions of the New Testament

| Gospels (4) |
| History (1) |
| Paul's letters (14) |
| General letters (7) |
| Prophecy (1) |

The Bible has two parts: the Old and the New Testament. *Testament* means a covenant or promise, an agreement between God and people.

Write the divisions on the lines below.

1. _______________: Matthew, Mark, Luke, John

2. _______________: Acts

3. _______________ _______________: Romans, 1 and 2 Corinthians, Galatians, Ephesians, Philippians, Colossians, 1 and 2 Thessalonians, 1 and 2 Timothy, Titus, Philemon, Hebrews.

4. _______________ _______________: James; 1 and 2 Peter; 1, 2, and 3 John; Jude.

5. _______________: Revelation

Scrambled Books

These books are out of order. Place each in the correct division with a check mark. The first one is done for you.

	Gospels	History	Paul's Letters	General Letters	Prophecy
1. Titus			✔		
2. John					
3. Acts					
4. James					
5. Ephesians					
6. Matthew					
7. Revelation					
8. Hebrews					
9. 2 Timothy					
10. Mark					
11. Jude					
12. Romans					

READ: Hebrews 8:7-10,13; 9:1,11,15; 13:20-21.

Gospels

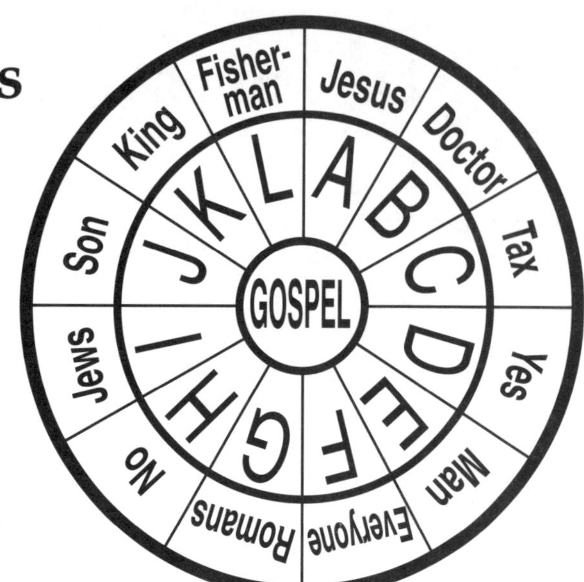

GOSPEL means GOOD NEWS.

Use the Gospel Wheel to complete the following statements and the chart.

The Gospels tell what ______________ was, what He said, and what He did. The Gospels is the good
         A

news of Jesus' coming, His life on earth, and His death on the cross. ______________ died to provide
         A

forgiveness of sins to all who accept Him as their Saviour.

Book	Matthew	Mark	Luke	John
Writer	Matthew (Levi)	John Mark	Luke	John
Key verse	2:2	10:45	1:3-4	20:31
Description of writer	____ collector C	____ of Mary* J	____ B	____ L
One of the 12 disciples	____ D	____ H	____ H	____ D
Written to	____ I	____ G	Greeks	____ F
Shows Jesus as	(Son of David) ____ K	Servant	____ E	____ of God J
Jesus quotes from Old Testament	____ D	____ D	____ D	____ D

READ: The key verses given above.
*(Not the mother of Jesus.)

Matthew; Mark

Matthew

Use the words on the crown to complete the statements.

Key Word: fulfilled

______________ carried out the ______________ made in the Old Testament. Jesus was the promised

______________, meaning ______________. The promise says Jesus will be ______________ on the

throne of David.

Many words or events in Matthew are found in the Old Testament. Draw a line from each Matthew reference to its Old Testament quote.

Reference	Verse
Matthew 27:35	1. "My God, my God, why have you forsaken me?" (Psalm 22:1a)
Matthew 27:46	2. "See, I will send my messenger, who will prepare the way before me." (Malachi 3:1a)
Matthew 11:10	3. "But you, Bethlehem . . . out of you will come for me one who will be ruler over Israel . . . ." (Micah 5:2a)
Matthew 2:5,6	4. "They divide my garments among them and cast lots for my clothing." (Psalm 22:18)

Mark

Key Word: immediately

Mark 1:18,20; 6:45,50; 9:20,24; 14:45. These Bible verses contain some words that mean the same as the key word. Write them below.

____

READ: Matthew 7:24-26; Mark 4:14-20.

Luke; John

Complete the puzzle to discover why Jesus came to earth.
Read Luke 19:10 to find the missing words.

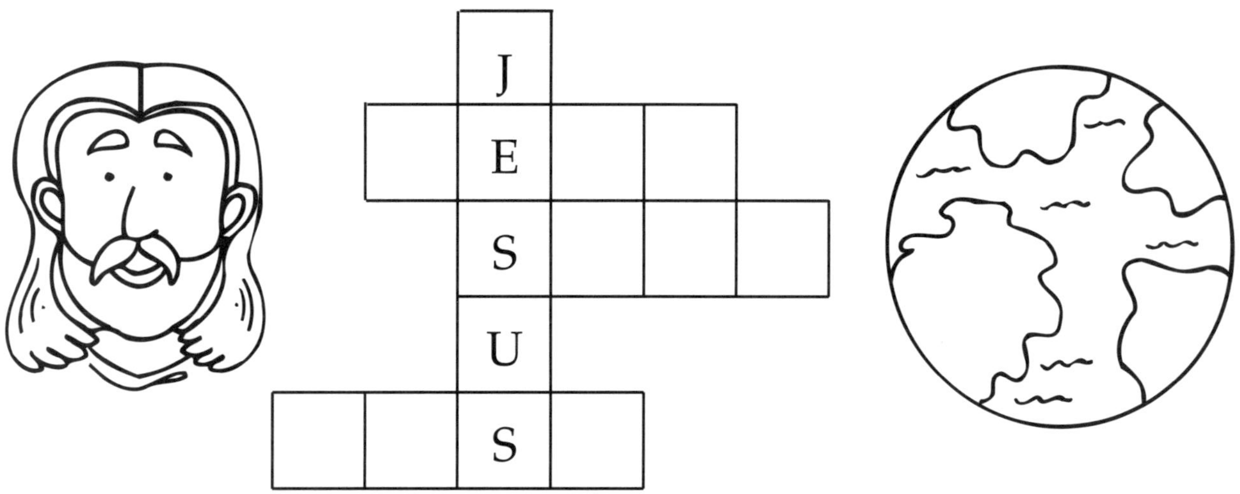

Luke shows that Jesus is a person and knows how we feel.

John—Key Word: Believe

John shows that Jesus is God's Son and can save us from sin.

Look up these Bible verses and add the missing words.

"For God so _____________ the _____________ that he gave his one and only _____________,

that whoever _____________ in him shall not _____________ but have _____________

_____________ ." (John 3:16)

". . . these are _____________ that you may _____________ that Jesus is the _____________, the

_____________ of God, and that by _____________ you may have _____________ in his name. "

(John 20:31)

Read each Bible verse; then draw a line from the kind of power to the Bible verse that refers to it.

Power

1. Power to heal	John 17:2
2. Power to forgive sins	Matthew 9:6
3. Power to lay down His life	Luke 6:19
4. Power to give eternal life	Luke 8:25
5. Power over nature	John 10:17-18

READ: Luke 6:17-19; 24:44-49; John 20:31.

Acts

Acts is the history of the early church. Luke wrote the Book of Acts as well as the Book of Luke.

Unscramble the names. Read the Bible verses if you need help.

1. T E R E P   _________________________ Acts 1:15

2. P T E H N E S   _________________________ Acts 7:55

3. H L I P I P   _________________________ Acts 8:30

4. R B N A B A S A   _________________________ Acts 11:22

5. U P A L   _________________________ Acts 13:16

6. L I S S A   _________________________ Acts 15:40

KEY VERSE: Cross out the letters F K X Z to find the key verse in Acts. Who made this statement?

```
Z K Y O U X W I L L F R E C E I V E
K X P O W E R X W H E N Z T H E K X
X H O L Y F S P I R I T F C O M E S
Z X O N F Y O U K A N D F Y O U X K
K X Z F W I L L K B E X M Y F X Z K
X Z K W I T N E S S E S K I N X Z Z
Z J E R U S A L E M F A N D Z I N X
X X F A L L F J U D E A K A N D X K
S A M A R I A X A N D Z T O F T H E
E N D S K O F X T H E Z E A R T H X
```

READ: Matthew 28:17-20; Acts 1:8-11; 28:30-31.

Romans; 1 and 2 Corinthians

	Romans
P	1 Corinthians
A	2 Corinthians
U	Galatians
L'	Ephesians
S	Philippians
	Colossians
L	1 Thessalonians
E	2 Thessalonians
T	1 Timothy
T	2 Timothy
E	Titus
R	Philemon
S	Hebrews

Paul wrote fourteen letters, called epistles.

Complete some of Paul's statements by writing one of these letters on each line: A E I O U

1. "F __ r __ ll h __ v __   s __ nned __ nd f__ ll sh __ rt __ f th __   gl __ ry __f

   G __ d." (Romans 3:23)

2. "__ v __ ry __ n __   wh __   c __ lls __ n th __ n __ m __   __ f th __   L __ rd

   w __ ll b __   s __ v __ d." (Romans 10:13)

3. ". . . Chr __ st d __ __ d f __ r __ __ r s __ ns __ cc __ rd __ ng t __   th __

   Scr __ pt __ r __ __ , th __ t h __   w __ s b __ r __ __ d, th __ t h __ w __ s

   r __ __ s __ d __ n th __   th __ rd d __ y. . . ." (1 Corinthians 15:3b-4)

Rearrange the following to make Bible verses. Check your work by looking up the verses in your Bible.

4. "We by live faith, by sight not." (2 Corinthians 5:7) _______________________________________

____

5. ". . . if in is anyone Christ, is new he a creation; the gone old has, has new the come!" (2 Corinthians 5:17)

____

____

READ: Romans 3:21-26; 1 Corinthians 15:3-4; 2 Corinthians 5:20-21.

    0-382-30701-1

Galatians; Ephesians

	Romans
P	1 Corinthians
A	2 Corinthians
U	Galatians
L'	Ephesians
S	Philippians
	Colossians
L	1 Thessalonians
E	2 Thessalonians
T	1 Timothy
T	2 Timothy
E	Titus
R	Philemon
S	Hebrews

Beginning at the star, write the words you pass on the lines below.

The main idea in Galatians is ________________ ________________ ________________.

The main idea in Ephesians is ________________ ________________ ________________.

Lessons From Galatians

Find the missing words by looking up the Bible references.

1. We are born into God's family by ________________ in Jesus Christ, not by things we do. (Galatians 3:26-27)

2. The ________________ is promised to God's children. (Galatians 3:14)

3. Christians should ________________ ________________ to everyone. (Galatians 6:10)

Lessons From Ephesians

4. Believers in Christ are saved by ________________. (Ephesians 2:8)

5. Believers in Christ are not saved by ________________. (Ephesians 2:9)

6. Who is the enemy of the believer? ________________ (Ephesians 6:11)

7. Ephesians 6 lists the armor God gives believers to take us through temptation. The sword of the Spirit is the ________________ ________________ ________________. (Ephesians 6:17)

READ: John 8:36; Galatians 5:1,22-25; 6:10; Ephesians 2:8-9; 4:32.

Philippians; Colossians

<table>
<tr><td>P</td><td>Romans</td></tr>
<tr><td>A</td><td>1 Corinthians</td></tr>
<tr><td>U</td><td>2 Corinthians</td></tr>
<tr><td>L'</td><td>Galatians</td></tr>
<tr><td>S</td><td>Ephesians</td></tr>
<tr><td></td><td>Philippians</td></tr>
<tr><td>L</td><td>Colossians</td></tr>
<tr><td>E</td><td>1 Thessalonians</td></tr>
<tr><td>T</td><td>2 Thessalonians</td></tr>
<tr><td>T</td><td>1 Timothy</td></tr>
<tr><td>E</td><td>2 Timothy</td></tr>
<tr><td>R</td><td>Titus</td></tr>
<tr><td>S</td><td>Philemon</td></tr>
<tr><td></td><td>Hebrews</td></tr>
</table>

1 E	2 P	3 C	1 P	4 P
4 H	1 H	2 H	4 I	2 I
4 L	3 O	4 E	1 E	4 M
2 L	1 S	2 I	2 P	2 P
3 L	2 I	1 I	2 A	2 N
4 O	1 A	3 O	1 N	4 N
3 S	3 S	1 S	3 I	3 A
3 N	3 S	2 S		

To find what Paul wrote while in a Roman prison, write the letters of the boxes with 1s on line 1. Do the same with 2, 3, and 4

1. ______________________________

2. ______________________________

3. ______________________________

4. ______________________________

Look up the Bible verses in Philippians and Colossians. Draw a line from each statement below to the verse that refers to it.

Lessons From Philippians

1. Paul's aim in life was to serve Jesus.   Philippians 4:13

2. We should follow the example of Jesus.   Philippians 1:21

3. Paul said Jesus helped him with everything.   Philippians 2:5

Lessons From Colossians

4. Jesus and God created everything.   Colossians 1:18a

5. Jesus is the head of the Church.   Colossians 1:16-17

6. We should do our best for God.   Colossians 1:23-24

READ: Philippians 2:5, 14-15; 4:12-13, 19. Colossians 2:6-7; 3:23-24

1 and 2 Thessalonians

To find what letters Paul wrote on his second missionary journey, write the letters for the boxes with 1s on line 1. Do the same with 2.

	Romans
P	1 Corinthians
A	2 Corinthians
U	Galatians
L'	Ephesians
S	Philippians
	Colossians
L	1 Thessalonians
E	2 Thessalonians
T	1 Timothy
T	2 Timothy
E	Titus
R	Philemon
S	Hebrews

1 F	2 S	1 I	2 E	1 R
2 C	2 O	1 S	2 N	2 D
1 T	2 T	1 T	2 H	1 H
2 E	1 E	2 S	1 S	1 S
2 S	1 A	2 A	1 L	2 L
1 O	2 O	1 N	2 N	2 I
2 A	1 I	2 N	1 A	1 N
1 S	2 S			

1. ______________ ____________________________

2. ______________ ____________________________

Rewrite the statement below, changing the spaces, to discover a wonderful surprise found in First and Second Thessalonians.

JESU SI SCOMIN GAG AIN!

____

What should Christians do while waiting for Jesus' return? Read the verses to find out. Write two words from each verse on the lines.

1. 1 Thessalonians 5:16 ____________ ____________

2. 1 Thessalonians 5:17 ____________ ____________

3. 1 Thessalonians 5:18 ____________ ____________

4. 1 Thessalonians 5:22 ____________ ____________

5. 2 Thessalonians 2:15 ____________ ____________

READ: 1 Thessalonians 4:7, 16-18; 5:2, 22; 2 Thessalonians 1:6-8; 3:3

     0-382-30701-1

1 and 2 Timothy; Titus

<table>
<tr><td>P</td><td>Romans</td></tr>
<tr><td>A</td><td>1 Corinthians</td></tr>
<tr><td>U</td><td>2 Corinthians</td></tr>
<tr><td>L'</td><td>Galatians</td></tr>
<tr><td>S</td><td>Ephesians</td></tr>
<tr><td></td><td>Philippians</td></tr>
<tr><td>L</td><td>Colossians</td></tr>
<tr><td>E</td><td>1 Thessalonians</td></tr>
<tr><td>T</td><td>2 Thessalonians</td></tr>
<tr><td>T</td><td>1 Timothy</td></tr>
<tr><td>E</td><td>2 Timothy</td></tr>
<tr><td>R</td><td>Titus</td></tr>
<tr><td>S</td><td>Philemon</td></tr>
<tr><td></td><td>Hebrews</td></tr>
</table>

Timothy or Titus?

Write *Timothy*, *Titus* or *Both* on each of the following lines.

1. Led to Christ by Paul ____
(1 Timothy 1:1-2; Titus 1:1,4)

2. Mother a Jew; father Greek _______________________________________
(Acts 16:1-3)

3. Worked with Paul ____

4. Taught the Scriptures by his mother and grandmother _______________________
(2 Timothy 1:5)

5. Visited Paul in prison _______________________________________
(Philippians 1:1,13)

Main Idea of 1 and 2 Timothy

Be _______________________ in _______________________ others.
(1 Thessalonians 5:24, word 7)　　(Matthew 28:20, word 2)

Main Ideas of Titus

_______________________ the _______________________ .
(Psalm 25:4, word 7)　　(John 6:47, word 5)

Jesus _______________________ so we can have _______________________
(1 Thessalonians 5:10, word 2)　　(John 6:47, last 2 words)

_______________________ .

READ: 1 Timothy 2:5-6a, 9-10; 2 Timothy 2:14-15, 24; Titus 2:11-12; 3:5.

Philemon; Hebrews

A	B	C	D	E	F	G	H	I	J	K	L	M
1	2	3	4	5	6	7	8	9	10	11	12	13

N	O	P	Q	R	S	T	U	V	W	X	Y	Z
14	15	16	17	18	19	20	21	22	23	24	25	26

Philemon

Use the code to complete this story.

Philemon, a __ __ __ __ __ __ of Paul, had a slave named Onesimus who __ __ __
6 18 9 5 14 4   18 1 14
__ __ __ __. Onesimus met __ __ __ __ and became a __ __ __ __ __ __ __ __ __ __
1 23 1 25   16 1 21 12   3 8 18 9 19 20 9 1 14
through Paul's teaching. Paul sent Onesimus back to his master with a __ __ __ __ __ __.
12 5 20 20 5 18
Paul asked Philemon to __ __ __ __ __ __ __ Onesimus. Paul also asked Philemon to
6 15 18 7 9 22 5
treat Onesimus as he would treat a fellow Christian even though Onesimus was a slave.

Hebrews

Jesus is better or superior. How is He better? Read the verses from Hebrews to find out; then complete the statements.

1. He is superior to the __ __ __ __ __ __ . (1:4)

2. He gives us a better __ __ __ __. (7:19)

3. He provides better and lasting __ __ __ __ __ __ __ __ __ __ , such as salvation. (10:34)

4. He will take us to a better __ __ __ __ __ __ __ . (11:16)

READ: Hebrews 1:1-2; 7:27; 8:13; 10:16-18; 11:1; Philemon 12,17.

James

<table>
<tr><td rowspan="8">G E N E R A L L E T T E R S</td></tr>
<tr><td>James</td></tr>
<tr><td>1 Peter</td></tr>
<tr><td>2 Peter</td></tr>
<tr><td>1 John</td></tr>
<tr><td>2 John</td></tr>
<tr><td>3 John</td></tr>
<tr><td>Jude</td></tr>
</table>

Key verse: 1:22

Complete the key verse and message by looking up words in other Bible verses.

"Do not merely _________________________ to the _________________________, and so deceive
                  (Isaiah 49:1, word 1)   (John 1:6, word 6)

yourselves. _________________________ what it says."
       (Galatians 6:10, word 8)

Message of James

_________________________ without _________________________ is dead.
   (Hebrews 11:17, word 2)   (Ephesians 2:9, word 3)

James wrote about the importance of "taming the tongue," or being careful of what we say. Circle words in the puzzle and write them on the lines to complete what James taught. Read James 3:3-8 if you need help.

We control _________________________ by

putting bits in their mouths. We control huge

_________________________ by turning small

_________________________. But we cannot

control our _________________________.

They often cause as much damage as a

_________________________. Our tongues are

full of _________________________.

```
S  R  R  N  Z  B  Q  L  Z
H  O  R  S  E  S  S  Y  B
I  J  K  U  V  W  F  B  L
P  Z  R  P  D  S  I  P  Q
S  D  G  O  L  D  R  Y  N
L  Q  U  I  Z  B  E  D  M
R  L  D  S  Z  V  T  R  R
Z  Y  T  O  N  G  U  E  S
N  O  R  N  C  D  G  J  K
```

READ: James 1:2-5; 2:20, 24; 4:7,10; 5:13,16.

1 and 2 Peter; 1, 2, and 3 John; Jude

G	James
E N E R A L	1 Peter
	2 Peter
	1 John
L E T T E R S	2 John
	3 John
	Jude

These books are all named after their authors.

Cross out each W and Z in the puzzle; then cross out the books of the Bible. Write the remaining letters on the lines to complete the message of each book.

1	Z	E	X	R	O	M	A	N	S	A	M	P	L	E
2	C	O	M	I	N	G	W	Z	W	A	G	A	I	N
3	M	Z	A	N	Z	A	W	N	D	Z	G	W	O	D
4	T	A	C	T	S	E	A	C	W	H	E	R	Z	S
5	D	W	O	A	M	O	S	G	Z	O	O	W	D	Z
6	T	J	O	H	N	E	A	C	Z	H	I	N	G	S

1. 1 Peter   Jesus is our ____ ____ ____ ____ ____ ____.

2. 2 Peter   Jesus is ____ ____ ____ ____ ____ ____   ____ ____ ____ ____.

3. 1 John   Jesus is both ____ ____ ____   ____ ____ ____   ____ ____ ____.

4. 2 John   Do not listen to false ____ ____ ____ ____ ____ ____ ____ ____.

5. 3 John   Imitate only those who ____ ____   ____ ____ ____ ____.

6. Jude   Defend the ____ ____ ____ ____ ____ ____ ____ ____ of Jesus.

READ: 1 Peter 3:17-18; 2 Peter 1:2-3; 1 John 1:9; 3:23-24; 2 John 7; 3 John 11; Jude 3.

      0-382-30701-1

Revelation

Fill in the squares with words that complete the sentences. Read the verses in Revelation if you need help.

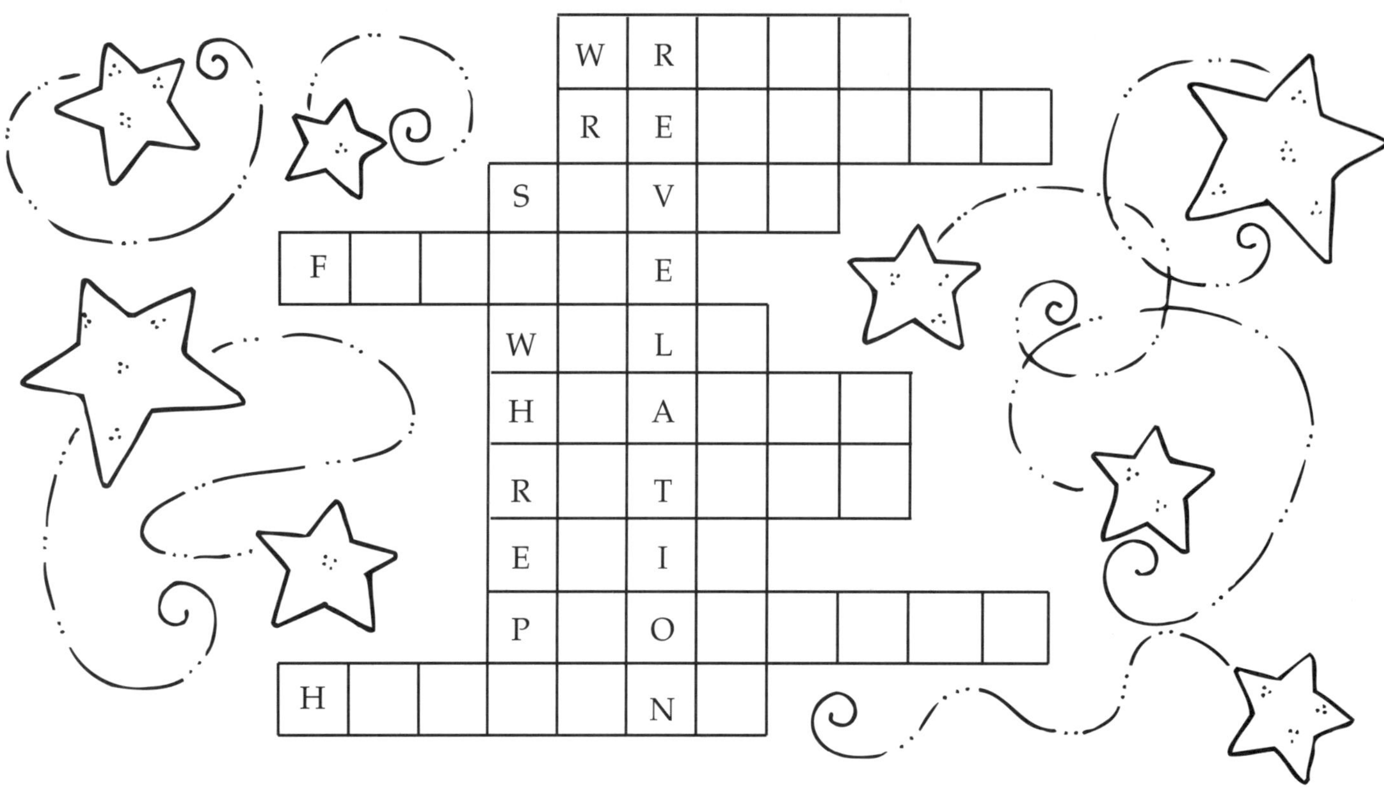

Jesus told John to _____________ His message in a book. (1:11, 19)
1

The message was given to _____________ churches. (1:11)
3

_____________ were promised to faithful followers.
2

God showed John the _____________.
4

John saw a picture of _____________.
6

Jesus will _____________ to earth. (1:5-7)
7

Jesus _____________ have victory over _____________.
5   8

This is a book of _____________. (word on this page)
9

Revelation tells what _____________ in the future.
10

READ: Revelation 1:9-11a; 3:20-22; 22:16, 19-21.

The Bible's Central Message

The message of the Bible is about one person. Find His name in John 20:31 and write it at the center of the wheel. Read the Bible verses outside the wheel. Match each one to the correct statement about Jesus. Write it on the correct line inside the wheel.

Isaiah 53:7

Galatians 3:16

Isaiah 25:9

Psalm 34:20

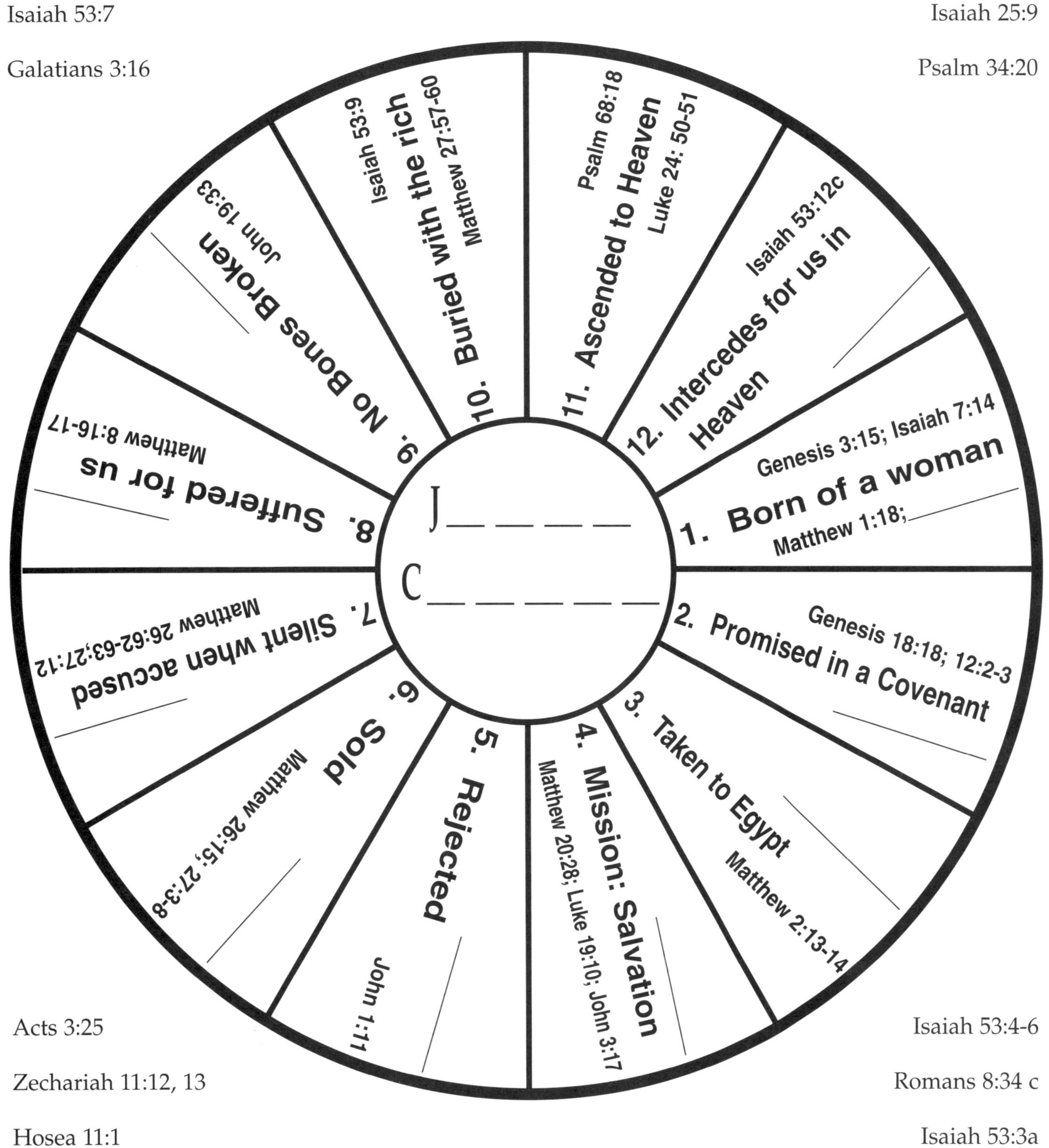

Acts 3:25

Zechariah 11:12, 13

Hosea 11:1

Isaiah 53:4-6

Romans 8:34 c

Isaiah 53:3a

Old Testament Book Search

Circle the books of the Old Testament.

```
M L A M E N T A T I O N S
A D C H R O N I C L E S R
L E S T H E R K I N G S U
A U J O S H U A E Z R A T
C T G E N E S I S J O B H
H E C C L E S I A S T E S
I R I   H H I J O N A H H
S O N G O F S O N G S   A
A N A E S A A E V E     G
M O M Z E D I L H I D D G
U M O E A A A K I N G S A
E Y S K E N H M I C A H I
L E V I T I C U S N   Y P
O X U E J E R E M I A H R
R O   L W L P S A L M S O
  D Z E P H A N I A H O V
N U M B E R S N A H U M E
R S Z E C H A R I A H D R
H A B A K K U K   I N   B
N E H E M I A H M Y H E S
O B A D I A H J U D G E S
          A R T
```

The remaining letters are a Bible verse. Write the words below.

"________ ________ ________ ________ ________ ________

________ ________ ." (Psalm 119:11a)

New Testament Book Search

Circle the books of the New Testament.

```
T  H  E  S  S  A  L  O  N  I  A  N  S
C  E  P  P  C  G  U  Y  O  A  C  T  S
O  B  H  H  O  A  K  T  I  T  U  S  U
R  R  E  I  L  L  E  R  O  M  A  N  S
I  E  S  L  O  A  R  W  J  A  M  E  S
N  W  I  I  S  T  O  R  D  J  O  H  N
T  S  A  P  S  I  M  A  T  T  H  E  W
H  I  N  P  I  A  S  A  L  M  A  R  K
I  A  S  I  A  N  T  I  M  O  T  H  Y
A  M  P  A  N  S  J  U  D  E  T  O  M
N  Y  F  N  S  P  H  I  L  E  M  O  N
S  E  E  S  T  P  E  T  E  R
R  E  V  E  L  A  T  I  O  N
```

The remaining letters are a Bible verse. Write the words below.

"Your ___________ ___________ ___________ ___________ ___________

___________ ___________." (Psalm 119:105a)

Bible Book Trivia

Write the letter of the correct answer on each line. If you need help, look up the Bible verse.

____	1. Number of chapters in the Bible	a. Numbers 7; 1 Chronicles 6; Luke 1
____	2. Number of chapters in the Old Testament	b. Psalm 70
____	3. Number of chapters in the New Testament	c. Psalm 117
____	4. Middle chapter in the Bible	d. Job 29
____	5. Middle chapter of the Old Testament	e. 929
____	6. Shortest chapter in the Bible	f. 2 Kings 19; Isaiah 37
____	7. Longest chapter in the Bible	g. Ezra 7:21
____	8. Second-longest chapter in the Bible	h. Numbers 7
____	9. Three chapters with 80 verses or more	i. John 11:35
____	10. Two chapters the most alike	j. Revelation 20:4
____	11. Two Psalms the most alike	k. Leviticus 25:10b
____	12. Psalm almost the same as Psalm 40:13-17	l. 1,189
____	13. Psalm with four verses almost alike	m. 260
____	14. Shortest verse in the Bible	n. Psalm 119
____	15. Shortest verse in the Old Testament	o. Esther 8:9
____	16. Longest verse in the Bible	p. 1 Chronicles 1:25
____	17. Longest verse in the New Testament	q. Psalms 14 & 53
____	18. A verse with all the letters of the alphabet except b, j, and q	r. Psalm 107: 8, 15, 21,
____	19. Bible verse written on the Liberty Bell	

Answer Key

Bible Library, page 4

Numbers
Ruth
2 Kings
Esther
Psalms
Jeremiah
Amos
Zephaniah
Malachi
Luke
1 Corinthians
2 Corinthians
1 Thessalonians
2 Thessalonians
Jude

First, Middle, and Last, page 5
Genesis, Psalms, Revelation

Chapters and Verses, page 7
31, 25, 24

1. C
2. F
3. A
4. B
5. E
6. D
7. Psalm 119:89
8. Revelation 14:13
9. Psalm 119:105, 130

Divisions of the Old Testament, page 8

1. Law
2. History
3. Poetry
4. Major Prophets
5. Minor Prophets

1. Minor Prophets
2. Law
3. Minor Prophets
4. History
5. Poetry
6. Major Prophets
7. Law
8. Minor Prophets
9. Major Prophet
10. Law
11. History
12. Poetry

Genesis, page 9
Beginning, Creation, Sin, Flood, Babel, Nation, Egypt

Exodus, page 10
going out, slavery, Moses, plagues, Passover, going out, Ten Commandments, tabernacle

Levitcus; Numbers, page 11
Laws
sacrifice and priesthood, number
A. Caleb
B. Joshua
obey, Canaan, forty

Numbers, page 12

Deuteronomy, page 13
Remember (used five times)
slaves, Egypt, God
God, Pharoah, Egypt
God, wilderness
covenant, God
sinned
Abraham
Egypt

Joshua; Judges; Ruth, page 14
Joshua: 3, 2, 1, 8, 5, 6, 7, 4
obeying, Word
Judges: disobeyed, defeated, prayed God
DEBORAH, GIDEON, SAMSON
Ruth: 5, 2, 4, 3, 1

1 and 2 Samuel, page 15

1. Samuel
   obey, sacrifice
2. Saul
3. David
4. Nathan
5. Jonathan
6. Absalom

1 and 2 Kings; 1 and 2 Chronicles, page 16

1. Israel, Judah
2. Solomon, Rehoboam, Jeroboam
3. 10
4. 2
5. Israel
6. Judah

page 17

7. Assyria
8. Hezekiah
9. Manasseh
10. Hezekiah
11. 586 B.C.
12. 70 years
13. 722 - 586 = 136 years

Ezra; Nehemiah; Esther, page 18

1. teacher
2. Law of Moses
3. God
4. Artaxerxes
5. 4 months
6. walls
7. gates
8. 52 days
9. Ezra
10. Mordecai
    Jesus Christ

Job, page 19

1. Satan, devil, power.
2. God, power, Satan.
3. God, send, trouble, Satan
4. God uses trouble, suffering, better person.

Psalms, page 20

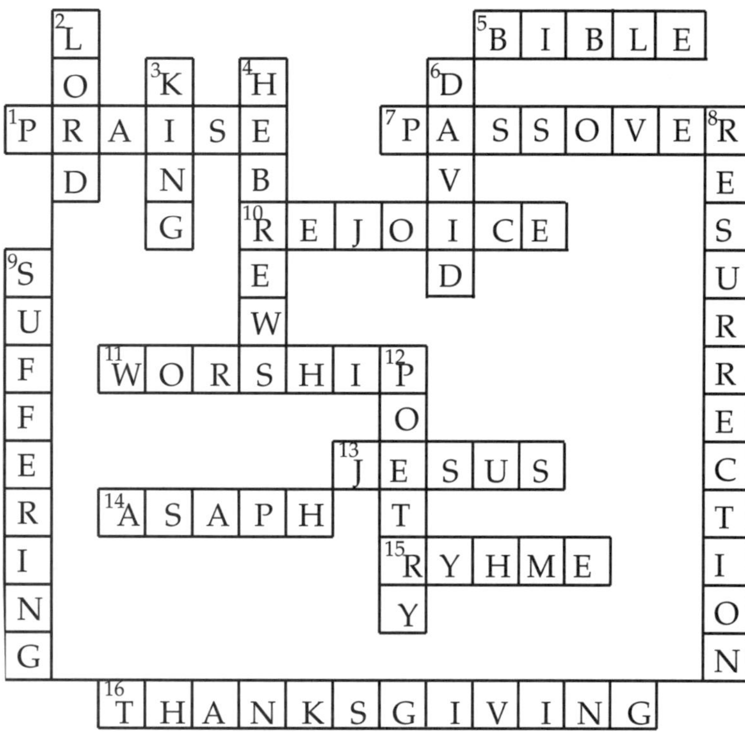

Proverbs; Ecclesiastes; Song of Solomon, page 21

1. A collection of wise sayings
2. A lesson from life. Obeying God is what really counts.
3. A love song written for his wife

Isaiah; Jeremiah; Lamentations, page 22

1. Isaiah 7:14; 9:6
2. Isaiah 11:1
3. Isaiah 11:2
4. Isaiah 11:5
5. Isaiah 53:5
6. Isaiah 25:8
7. Isaiah 32:1
8. Jeremiah 29:10
9. Jeremiah 32:37-38
10. Jeremiah 25:8-9
11. Jeremiah 31:31

Ezekiel; Daniel, page 23

ZHHAEIEK = Hezekiah

1. Jeremiah, Ezekiel, Daniel
2. 70
3. Josiah
4. Jehoiakim

Hosea; Joel; Amos; Obadiah, page 24

1. Amos
2. Amos
3. Hosea
4. Obadiah
5. Joel
6. Amos
7. Hosea
8. Amos
9. Joel

Jonah; Micah; Nahum; Habakkuk, page 25

1. Micah
2. Jonah
3. Nahum
4. Habakkuk
5. Jonah
6. Nahum
7. Habakkuk
8. Micah
9. Nahum
10. Habakkuk

Zephaniah; Haggai; Zechariah; Malachi, page 26

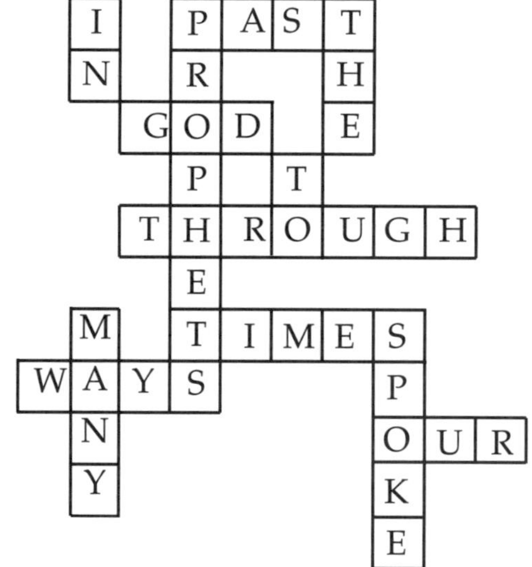

1. Zechariah, Malachi, Haggai
2. Malachi
3. Haggai
4. Zephaniah
5. 70
6. 12
7. 5

Divisions of the New Testament, page 27

1. Gospels
2. History
3. Paul's Letters (Epistles)
4. General Letters (Epistles)
5. Prophecy

1. Paul's letters
2. Gospels
3. History
4. General letters
5. Paul's letters
6. Gospels
7. Prophecy
8. Paul's letters
9. Paul's letters
10. Gospels
11. General letters
12. Paul's letters

Gospels, page 28
Jesus, Jesus

Matthew	Mark	Luke	John
tax	son	doctor	fisherman
yes	no	no	yes
Jews	Romans	man	everyone
King	yes	yes	Son
yes			yes

Matthew; Mark, page 29

Jesus	1. Matthew 27:46
promises	2. Matthew 11:10
Messiah	3. Matthew 2:5,6
Saviour	4. Matthew 27:35
King	at once, without delay, immediately

Luke; John, page 30
seek, save, lost
loved, world, Son, believes, perish, eternal life.
Written, believe, Christ, Son, believing, life.
1. Luke 6:19
2. Matthew 9:6
3. John 10:17-18
4. John 17:2
5. Luke 8:25

Acts, page 31
1. Peter
2. Stephen
3. Philip
4. Barnabas
5. Paul
6. Silas

```
    Y O U   W I L L   R E C E I V E
    P O W E R   W H E N   T H E
  H O L Y   S P I R I T   C O M E S
    O N   Y O U   A N D   Y O U
        W I L L   B E   M Y
      W I T N E S S E S   I N
  J E R U S A L E M   A N D   I N
      A L L   J U D E A   A N D
S A M A R I A   A N D   T O   T H E
E N D S   O F   T H E   E A R T H
```

Romans; 1 and 2 Corinthians, page 32
1. "For all have sinned and fall short of the glory of God."
2. "Everyone who calls on the name of the Lord will be saved."
3. ". . . Christ died for our sins according to the Scriptures, that he was buried, that he was raised on the third day . . . ."
4. "We live by faith, not by sight."
5. "If anyone is in Christ, he is a new creation; the old has gone, the new has come!"

Galatians; Ephesians, page 33
Free from law
Saved by grace
1. faith
2. Spirit (Holy Spirit)
3. do good
4. grace
5. works
6. the devil
7. the Word of God (Bible)

Philippians; Colossians, page 34
1. Ephesians
2. Philippians
3. Colossians
4. Philemon
1. Phillipians 1:21
2. Phillipians 2:5
3. Phillipians 4:13
4. Colossians 1:16-17
5. Colossians 1:18a
6. Colossians 1:23-24

1 and 2 Thessalonians, page 35
1. First Thessalonians.
2. Second Thessalonians
Jesus is coming again!
1. Be joyful
2. Pray continually
3. Give thanks
4. Avoid evil
5. Stand firm

1 and 2 Timothy; Titus, page 36
1. both
2. Timothy
3. both
4. Timothy
5. Timothy

faithful, teaching
teach, truth
died, everlasting life

Philemon; Hebrews, page 37

friend	1. angels
ran away	2. hope
Paul	3. possessions
Christian	4. country
letter	
forgive	

James, page 38

listen, word, Do   Faith, works

```
S  R  R  N  Z  B  Q  L  Z
H  O  R  S  E  S  S  Y  B
I  J  K  U  V  W  F  B  L
P  Z  R  P  D  S  I  P  Q
S  D  G  O  L  D  R  Y  N
L  Q  U  I  Z  B  E  D  M
R  L  D  S  Z  V  T  R  R
Z  Y  T  O  N  G  U  E  S
N  O  R  N  C  D  G  J  K
```

1 and 2 Peter; 1, 2, and 3 John; Jude, page 39

1. example
2. coming again
3. man and God
4. teachers
5. do good
6. teachings

Revelation, page 40

1. write	6. Heaven
2. Rewards	7. return
3. seven	8. evil
4. future	9. prophecy
5. will	10. happens

The Bible's Message, page 41

Jesus Christ	6. Zechariah 11:12,13
1. Galatians 3:16	7. Isaiah 53:7
2. Acts 3:25	8. Isaiah 53:4-6
3. Hosea 11:1	9. Psalm 34:20
4. Isaiah 25:9	12. Romans 8:34c
5. Isaiah 53:3a	

Old Testament Book Search, page 42

```
M  L  A  M  E  N  T  A  T  I  O  N  S
A  D  C  H  R  O  N  I  C  L  E  S  R
L  E  S  T  H  E  R  K  I  N  G  S  U
A  U  J  O  S  H  U  A  E  Z  R  A  T
C  T  G  E  N  E  S  I  S  J  O  B  H
H  E  C  C  L  E  S  I  A  S  T  E  S
I  R  I  H  H  I  J  O  N  A  H  H
S  O  N  G  O  F  S  O  N  G  S  G
A  N  A  E  S  A  A  E  V  E  G
M  O  M  Z  E  D  I  L  H  I  D  D  G
U  M  O  E  A  A  A  K  I  N  G  S  A
E  Y  S  K  E  N  H  M  I  C  A  H  I
L  E  V  I  T  I  C  U  S  N  Y  P
O  X  U  E  J  E  R  E  M  I  A  H  R
R  O  L  W  L  P  S  A  L  M  S  O
D  Z  E  P  H  A  N  I  A  H  O  V
N  U  M  B  E  R  S  N  A  H  U  M  E
R  S  Z  E  C  H  A  R  I  A  H  D  R
H  A  B  A  K  K  U  K  I  N  B
N  E  H  E  M  I  A  H  M  Y  H  E  S
O  B  A  D  I  A  H  J  U  D  G  E  S
         A  R  T
```

"I have hidden your word in my heart."

New Testament Book Search, page 43

```
T  H  E  S  S  A  L  O  N  I  A  N  S
C  E  P  P  C  G  U  Y  O  A  C  T  S
O  B  H  H  O  A  K  E  T  I  T  U  S
R  R  E  I  L  L  E  R  O  M  A  N  S
I  E  S  L  O  A  R  W  J  A  M  E  S
N  W  I  I  S  T  O  R  D  J  O  H  N
T  S  A  P  S  I  M  A  T  T  H  E  W
H  I  N  P  I  A  S  A  L  M  A  R  K
I  A  S  I  A  N  T  I  M  O  T  H  Y
A  M  P  A  N  S  J  U  D  E  T  O  M
N  Y  F  N  S  P  H  I  L  E  M  O  N
S  E  E  S  T  P  E  T  E  R
R  E  V  E  L  A  T  I  O  N
```

"Your word is a lamp to my feet."

Bible Book Trivia, page 44

1. L	2. E	3. M	4. C	5. D	6. C	7. N
8. H	9. A	10. F	11. Q,	12. B	13. R	
14. I	15. P	16. O	17. J	18. G	19. K	